THE
METAMORPHOSIS

FRANZ KAFKA

THE METAMORPHOSIS
by Franz Kafka
Translated by Ian Johnston

Published by Tribeca Books
ISBN 978-1936594009
Printed in the USA

Cover Design by Tribeca Books

1

One morning, as Gregor Samsa was waking up from anxious dreams, he discovered that in bed he had been changed into a monstrous verminous bug. He lay on his armour-hard back and saw, as he lifted his head up a little, his brown, arched abdomen divided up into rigid bow-like sections. From this height the blanket, just about ready to slide off completely, could hardly stay in place. His numerous legs, pitifully thin in comparison to the rest of his circumference, flickered helplessly before his eyes.

"What's happened to me," he thought. It was no dream. His room, a proper room for a human being, only somewhat too small, lay quietly between the four well-known walls. Above the table, on which an unpacked collection of sample cloth goods was spread out (Samsa was a traveling salesman) hung the picture which he had cut out of an illustrated magazine a little while ago and set in a pretty gilt frame. It was a picture of a woman with a fur hat and a fur boa. She sat erect there, lifting up in the direction of the viewer a solid fur muff into which her entire forearm disappeared.

Gregor's glance then turned to the window. The dreary weather (the rain drops were falling audibly down on the metal window ledge) made him quite melancholy. "Why don't I keep sleeping for a little while longer and forget all this foolishness," he thought. But this was entirely impractical, for he was used to sleeping on his right side, and in his present state he couldn't get himself into this position. No matter how hard he threw himself onto his right side, he always rolled again onto his back. He must have tried it a hundred times, closing his eyes, so that he would not have to see the wriggling legs, and gave up only when he began to feel a light, dull pain in his side which he had never felt before.

"O God," he thought, "what a demanding job I've chosen! Day in, day out on the road. The stresses of trade are much greater than the work going on at head office, and, in addition to that, I have to deal with the problems of traveling, the worries about train connections, irregular bad food, temporary and constantly changing human relationships which never come from the heart. To hell with it all!" He felt a slight itching on the top of his abdomen. He slowly pushed himself on his back closer to the bed post so that he could lift his head more easily, found the itchy part, which was entirely covered with small white spots (he did not know what to make of them), and wanted to feel the place with a leg. But he retracted it immediately, for the contact felt like a cold shower all over him.

He slid back again into his earlier position. "This getting up early," he thought, "makes a man quite idiotic. A man must have his sleep. Other traveling salesmen live like harem women. For instance, when I come back to the inn during the course of the morning to write up the necessary orders, these gentlemen are just sitting down to breakfast. If I were to try that with my boss, I'd be thrown out on the spot. Still, who knows whether that mightn't be really good for me. If I didn't hold back for my parents' sake, I would've quit ages ago. I would've gone to the boss and told him just what I think from the bottom of my heart. He would've fallen right off his desk! How weird it is to sit up at the desk and talk down to the employee from way up there. The boss has trouble hearing, so the employee has to step up quite close to him. Anyway, I haven't completely given up that hope yet. Once I've got together the money to pay off the parents' debt to him-- that should take another five or six years--I'll do it for sure. Then I'll make the big break. In any case, right now I have to get up. My train leaves at five o'clock."

And he looked over at the alarm clock ticking away by the chest of drawers. "Good God," he thought. It was half past six, and the hands were going quietly on. It was past the half hour, already nearly quarter to. Could the alarm have failed to ring? One saw from the bed that it was properly set for four o'clock. Certainly it had rung. Yes, but was it possible to sleep through this noise that made the furniture shake? Now, it's true he'd not slept quietly, but evidently he'd slept all the more deeply. Still, what should he do now? The next train left at seven o'clock. To catch that one, he would have to go in a mad rush. The sample collection wasn't packed up yet, and he really didn't feel particularly fresh and active. And even if he caught the train, there was no avoiding a blow up with the boss, because the firm's errand boy would've waited for the five o'clock train and reported the news of his absence long ago. He was the boss's minion, without backbone or intelligence. Well then, what if he reported in sick? But that would be extremely embarrassing and suspicious, because during his five years' service Gregor hadn't been sick even once. The boss would certainly come with the doctor from the health insurance company and would reproach his parents for their lazy son and cut short all objections with the insurance doctor's comments; for him everyone was completely healthy but really lazy about work. And besides, would the doctor in this case be totally wrong? Apart from a really excessive drowsiness after the long sleep, Gregor in fact felt quite well and even had a really strong appetite.

As he was thinking all this over in the greatest haste, without being able to make the decision to get out of bed (the alarm clock was indicating exactly quarter to seven) there was a cautious knock on the door by the head of the bed.

"Gregor," a voice called (it was his mother!) "it's quarter to seven. Don't you want to be on your way?" The soft voice! Gregor was startled when he heard his voice answering. It was clearly and unmistakably his earlier voice, but in it was intermingled, as if from below, an irrepressibly painful squeaking which left the words positively distinct only in the first moment and distorted them in the reverberation, so that one didn't know if one had heard correctly. Gregor wanted to answer in detail and explain everything, but in these circumstances he confined himself to saying, "Yes, yes, thank you mother. I'm getting up right away." Because of the wooden door the change in Gregor's voice was not really noticeable outside, so his mother calmed down with this explanation and shuffled off. However, as a result of the short conversation the other family members became aware of the fact that Gregor was unexpectedly still at home, and already his father was knocking on one side door, weakly but with his fist. "Gregor, Gregor," he called out, "what's going on?" And after a short while he urged him on again in a deeper voice. "Gregor!" Gregor!" At the other side door, however, his sister knocked lightly. "Gregor? Are you all right? Do you need anything?" Gregor directed answers in both directions, "I'll be ready right away." He made an effort with the most careful articulation and by inserting long pauses between the individual words to remove everything remarkable from his voice. His father turned back to his breakfast. However, the sister whispered, "Gregor, open the door, I beg you." Gregor had no intention of opening the door, but congratulated himself on his precaution, acquired from traveling, of locking all doors during the night, even at home.

First he wanted to stand up quietly and undisturbed, get dressed, above all have breakfast, and only then consider further action, for (he noticed this clearly) by thinking things over in bed he would not reach a reasonable conclusion. He remembered that he had already often felt a light pain or other in bed, perhaps the result of an awkward lying position, which later turned out to be purely imaginary when he stood up, and he was eager to see how his present fantasies would gradually dissipate. That the change in his voice was nothing other than the onset of a real chill, an occupational illness of commercial travelers, of that he had not the slightest doubt.

It was very easy to throw aside the blanket. He needed only to push himself up a little, and it fell by itself. But to continue was difficult, particularly because he was so unusually wide. He needed arms and hands to push himself upright. Instead of these, however, he had only many small limbs which were incessantly moving with very different motions and which, in addition, he was unable to control. If he wanted to bend one of them, then it was the first to extend itself, and if he finally succeeded doing with this limb what he wanted, in the meantime all the others, as if left free, moved around in an excessively painful agitation. "But I must not stay in bed uselessly," said Gregor to himself.

At first he wanted to get of the bed with the lower part of his body, but this lower part (which he incidentally had not yet looked at and which he also couldn't picture clearly) proved itself too difficult to move. The attempt went so slowly. When, having become almost frantic, he finally hurled himself forward with all his force and without thinking, he chose his direction incorrectly, and he hit the lower bedpost hard. The violent pain he felt revealed to him that the lower part of his body was at the moment probably the most sensitive.

Thus, he tried to get his upper body out of the bed first and turned his head carefully toward the edge of the bed. He managed to do this easily, and in spite of its width and weight his body mass at last slowly followed the turning of his head. But as he finally raised his head outside the bed in the open air, he became anxious about moving forward any further in this manner, for if he allowed himself eventually to fall by this process, it would take a miracle to prevent his head from getting injured. And at all costs he must not lose consciousness right now. He preferred to remain in bed.

However, after a similar effort, while he lay there again sighing as before and once again saw his small limbs fighting one another, if anything worse than before, and didn't see any chance of imposing quiet and order on this arbitrary movement, he told himself again that he couldn't possibly remain in bed and that it might be the most reasonable thing to sacrifice everything if there was even the slightest hope of getting himself out of bed in the process. At the same moment, however, he didn't forget to remind himself from time to time of the fact that calm (indeed the calmest) reflection might be better than the most confused decisions. At such moments, he directed his gaze as precisely as he could toward the window, but unfortunately there was little confident cheer to be had from a glance at the morning mist, which concealed even the other side of the narrow street. "It's already seven o'clock" he told himself at the latest striking of the alarm clock, "already seven o'clock and still such a fog." And for a little while longer he lay quietly with weak breathing, as if perhaps waiting for normal and natural conditions to re-emerge out of the complete stillness.

But then he said to himself, "Before it strikes a quarter past seven, whatever happens I must be completely out of bed. Besides, by then someone from the office will arrive to inquire about me, because the office will open before seven o'clock." And he made an effort then to rock his entire body length out of the bed with a uniform motion. If he let himself fall out of the bed in this way, his head, which in the course of the fall he intended to lift up sharply, would probably remain uninjured. His back seemed to be hard; nothing would really happen to that as a result of the fall. His greatest reservation was a worry about the loud noise which the fall must create and which presumably would arouse, if not fright, then at least concern on the other side of all the doors. However, it had to be tried.

As Gregor was in the process of lifting himself half out of bed (the new method was more of a game than an effort; he needed only to rock with a constant rhythm) it struck him how easy all this would be if someone were to come to his aid. Two strong people (he thought of his father and the servant girl) would have been quite sufficient. They would have only had to push their arms under his arched back to get him out of the bed, to bend down with their load, and then merely to exercise patience and care that he completed the flip onto the floor, where his diminutive legs would then, he hoped, acquire a purpose. Now, quite apart from the fact that the doors were locked, should he really call out for help? In spite of all his distress, he was unable to suppress a smile at this idea.

He had already got to the point where, with a stronger rocking, he maintained his equilibrium with difficulty, and very soon he would finally have to decide, for in five minutes it would be a quarter past seven. Then there was a ring at the door of the apartment. "That's someone from the office" he told himself, and he almost froze while his small limbs only danced around all the faster. For one moment everything remained still. "They aren't opening," Gregor said to himself, caught up in some absurd hope. But of course then, as usual, the servant girl with her firm tread went to the door and opened it. Gregor needed to hear only the visitor's first word of greeting to recognize immediately who it was, the manager himself. Why was Gregor the only one condemned to work in a firm where at the slightest lapse someone immediately attracted the greatest suspicion? Were all the employees then collectively, one and all, scoundrels? Was there then among them no truly devoted person who, if he failed to use just a couple of hours in the morning for office work, would become abnormal from pangs of conscience and really be in no state to get out of bed? Was it really not enough to let an apprentice make inquiries, if such questioning was even necessary? Must the manager himself come, and in the process must it be demonstrated to the entire innocent family that the investigation of this suspicious circumstance could only be entrusted to the intelligence of the manager? And more as a consequence of the excited state in which this idea put Gregor than as a result of an actual decision, he swung himself with all his might out of the bed. There was a loud thud, but not a real crash. The fall was absorbed somewhat by the carpet and, in addition, his back was more elastic than Gregor had thought. For that reason the dull noise was not quite so conspicuous. But he had not held his head up with sufficient care and had hit it. He turned his head, irritated and in pain, and rubbed it on the carpet.

"Something has fallen in there," said the manager in the next room on the left. Gregor tried to imagine to himself whether anything similar to what was happening to him today could have also happened at some point to the manager. At least one had to concede the possibility of such a thing. However, as if to give a rough answer to this question, the manager now took a few determined steps in the next room, with a squeak of his polished boots. From the neighbouring room on the right the sister was whispering to inform Gregor: "Gregor, the manager is here." "I know," said Gregor to himself. But he did not dare make his voice loud enough so that his sister could hear.

"Gregor," his father now said from the neighbouring room on the left, "Mr. Manager has come and is asking why you have not left on the early train. We don't know what we should tell him. Besides, he also wants to speak to you personally. So please open the door. He will be good enough to forgive the mess in your room."

In the middle of all this, the manager called out in a friendly way, "Good morning, Mr. Samsa." "He is not well," said his mother to the manager, while his father was still talking at the door, "He is not well, believe me, Mr. Manager. Otherwise how would Gregor miss a train! The young man has nothing in his head except business. I'm almost angry that he never goes out at night. Right now he's been in the city eight days, but he's been at home every evening. He sits there with us at the table and reads the newspaper quietly or studies his travel schedules. It's quite a diversion for him if he busies himself with fretwork. For instance, he cut out a small frame over the course of two or three evenings. You'd be amazed how pretty it is. It's hanging right inside the room. You'll see it immediately, as soon as Gregor opens the door. Anyway, I'm happy that you're here, Mr. Manager. By ourselves, we would never have made Gregor open the door. He's so stubborn, and he's certainly not well, although he denied that this morning."

"I'm coming right away," said Gregor slowly and deliberately and didn't move, so as not to lose one word of the conversation. "My dear lady, I cannot explain it to myself in any other way," said the manager; "I hope it is nothing serious. On the other hand, I must also say that we business people, luckily or unluckily, however one looks at it, very often simply have to overcome a slight indisposition for business reasons." "So can Mr. Manager come in to see you now" asked his father impatiently and knocked once again on the door. "No," said Gregor. In the neighbouring room on the left a painful stillness descended. In the neighbouring room on the right the sister began to sob.

Why didn't his sister go to the others? She'd probably just gotten up out of bed now and hadn't even started to get dressed yet. Then why was she crying? Because he wasn't getting up and wasn't letting the manager in; because he was in danger of losing his position, and because then his boss would badger his parents once again with the old demands? Those were probably unnecessary worries right now. Gregor was still here and wasn't thinking at all about abandoning his family. At the moment he was lying right there on the carpet, and no one who knew about his condition would've seriously demanded that he let the manager in. But Gregor wouldn't be casually dismissed right way because of this small discourtesy, for which he would find an easy and suitable excuse later on. It seemed to Gregor that it might be far more reasonable to leave him in peace at the moment, instead of disturbing him with crying and conversation. But it was the very uncertainty which distressed the others and excused their behaviour.

"Mr. Samsa," the manager was now shouting, his voice raised, "what's the matter? You are barricading yourself in your room, answer with only a yes and a no, are making serious and unnecessary troubles for your parents, and neglecting (I mention this only incidentally) your commercial duties in a truly unheard of manner. I am speaking here in the name of your parents and your employer, and I am requesting you in all seriousness for an immediate and clear explanation. I am amazed. I am amazed. I thought I knew you as a calm, reasonable person, and now you appear suddenly to want to start parading around in weird moods. The Chief indicated to me earlier this very day a possible explanation for your neglect--it concerned the collection of cash entrusted to you a short while ago--but in truth I almost gave him my word of honour that this explanation could not be correct. However, now I see here your unimaginable pig headedness, and I am totally losing any desire to speak up for you in the slightest. And your position is not at all the most secure. Originally I intended to mention all this to you privately, but since you are letting me waste my time here uselessly, I don't know why the matter shouldn't come to the attention of your parents. Your productivity has also been very unsatisfactory recently. Of course, it's not the time of year to conduct exceptional business, we recognize that, but a time of year for conducting no business, there is no such thing at all, Mr. Samsa, and such a thing must never be."

"But Mr. Manager," called Gregor, beside himself and in his agitation forgetting everything else, "I'm opening the door immediately, this very moment. A slight indisposition, a dizzy spell, has prevented me from getting up. I'm still lying in bed right now. But now I'm quite refreshed once again. I'm in the midst of getting out of bed. Just have patience for a short moment! Things are not going so well as I thought. But things are all right. How suddenly this can overcome someone! Just yesterday evening everything was fine with me. My parents certainly know that. Actually just yesterday evening I had a small premonition. People must have seen that in me. Why have I not reported that to the office! But people always think that they'll get over sickness without having to stay at home. Mr. Manager! Take it easy on my parents! There is really no basis for the criticisms which you are now making against me, and really nobody has said a word to me about that. Perhaps you have not read the latest orders which I shipped. Besides, now I'm setting out on my trip on the eight o'clock train; the few hours' rest have made me stronger. Mr. Manager, do not stay. I will be at the office in person right away. Please have the goodness to say that and to convey my respects to the Chief."

While Gregor was quickly blurting all this out, hardly aware of what he was saying, he had moved close to the chest of drawers without effort, probably as a result of the practice he had already had in bed, and now he was trying to raise himself up on it. Actually, he wanted to open the door; he really wanted to let himself be seen by and to speak with the manager. He was keen to witness what the others now asking after him would say at the sight of him. If they were startled, then Gregor had no more responsibility and could be calm. But if they accepted everything quietly, then he would have no reason to get excited and, if he got a move on, could really be at the station around eight o'clock.

At first he slid down a few times from the smooth chest of drawers. But at last he gave himself a final swing and stood upright there. He was no longer at all aware of the pains in his lower body, no matter how they might still sting. Now he let himself fall against the back of a nearby chair, on the edge of which he braced himself with his thin limbs. By doing this he gained control over himself and kept quiet, for he could now hear the manager.

"Did you understand a single word?" the manager asked the parents, "Is he playing the fool with us?" "For God's sake," cried the mother already in tears, "perhaps he's very ill and we're upsetting him. Grete! Grete!" she yelled at that point. "Mother?" called the sister from the other side. They were making themselves understood through Gregor's room. "You must go to the doctor right away. Gregor is sick. Hurry to the doctor. Have you heard Gregor speak yet?" "That was an animal's voice," said the manager, remarkably quietly in comparison to the mother's cries.

"Anna! Anna!' yelled the father through the hall into the kitchen, clapping his hands, "fetch a locksmith right away!" The two young women were already running through the hall with swishing skirts (how had his sister dressed herself so quickly?) and yanked open the doors of the apartment. One couldn't hear the doors closing at all. They probably had left them open, as is customary in an apartment in which a huge misfortune has taken place.

However, Gregor had become much calmer. All right, people did not understand his words any more, although they seemed clear enough to him, clearer than previously, perhaps because his ears had gotten used to them. But at least people now thought that things were not all right with him and were prepared to help him. The confidence and assurance with which the first arrangements had been carried out made him feel good. He felt himself included once again in the circle of humanity and was expecting from both the doctor and the locksmith, without differentiating between them with any real precision, splendid and surprising results. In order to get as clear a voice as possible for the critical conversation which was imminent, he coughed a little, and certainly took the trouble to do this in a really subdued way, since it was possible that even this noise sounded like something different from a human cough. He no longer trusted himself to decide any more. Meanwhile in the next room it had become really quiet. Perhaps his parents were sitting with the manager at the table and were whispering; perhaps they were all leaning against the door and listening.

Gregor pushed himself slowly towards the door, with the help of the easy chair, let go of it there, threw himself against the door, held himself upright against it (the balls of his tiny limbs had a little sticky stuff on them), and rested there momentarily from his exertion. Then he made an effort to turn the key in the lock with his mouth. Unfortunately it seemed that he had no real teeth. How then was he to grab hold of the key? But to make up for that his jaws were naturally very strong; with their help he managed to get the key really moving, and he did not notice that he was obviously inflicting some damage on himself, for a brown fluid came out of his mouth, flowed over the key, and dripped onto the floor.

"Just listen for a moment," said the manager in the next room, "he's turning the key." For Gregor that was a great encouragement. But they all should've called out to him, including his father and mother, "Come on, Gregor," they should've shouted, "keep going, keep working on the lock."

Imagining that all his efforts were being followed with suspense, he bit down frantically on the key with all the force he
could muster. As the key turned more, he danced around the
lock. Now he was holding himself upright only with his
mouth, and he had to hang onto the key or then press it
down again with the whole weight of his body, as necessary.
The quite distinct click of the lock as it finally snapped really
woke Gregor up. Breathing heavily he said to himself, "So I
didn't need the locksmith," and he set his head against the
door handle to open the door completely.

Because he had to open the door in this way, it was already
open very wide without him yet being really visible. He first
had to turn himself slowly around the edge of the door, very
carefully, of course, if he did not want to fall awkwardly on
his back right at the entrance into the room. He was still pre-
occupied with this difficult movement and had no time to pay
attention to anything else, when he heard the manager ex-
claim a loud "Oh!" (it sounded like the wind whistling), and
now he saw him, nearest to the door, pressing his hand
against his open mouth and moving slowly back, as if an invisible constant force was pushing him away. His mother (in
spite of the presence of the manager she was standing here
with her hair sticking up on end, still a mess from the night)
with her hands clasped was looking at his father; she then
went two steps towards Gregor and collapsed right in the
middle of her skirts spreading out all around her, her face
sunk on her breast, completely concealed. His father clenched
his fist with a hostile expression, as if he wished to push
Gregor back into his room, then looked uncertainly around
the living room, covered his eyes with his hands, and cried so

that his mighty breast shook.

At this point Gregor did not take one step into the room, but leaned his body from the inside against the firmly bolted wing of the door, so that only half his body was visible, as well as his head, titled sideways, with which he peeped over at the others. Meanwhile it had become much brighter. Standing out clearly from the other side of the street was a part of the endless gray-black house situated opposite (it was a hospital) with its severe regular windows breaking up the facade. The rain was still coming down, but only in large individual drops visibly and firmly thrown down one by one onto the ground. The breakfast dishes were standing piled around on the table, because for his father breakfast was the most important meal time in the day, which he prolonged for hours by reading various newspapers. Directly across on the opposite wall hung a photograph of Gregor from the time of his military service; it was a picture of him as a lieutenant, as he, smiling and worry free, with his hand on his sword, demanded respect for his bearing and uniform. The door to the hall was ajar, and since the door to the apartment was also open, one saw out into the landing of the apartment and the start of the staircase going down.

"Now," said Gregor, well aware that he was the only one who had kept his composure. "I'll get dressed right away, pack up the collection of samples, and set off. You'll allow me to set out on my way, will you not? You see, Mr. Manager, I am not pig-headed, and I am happy to work. Traveling is exhausting, but I couldn't live without it. Where are you going, Mr. Manager? To the office? Really? Will you report everything truthfully? A person can be incapable of work momentarily, but that is precisely the best time to remember the earlier achievements and to consider that later, after the obstacles have been shoved aside, the person will work all the more keenly and intensely. I am really so indebted to Mr. Chief--you know that perfectly well. On the other hand, I am concerned about my parents and my sister. I'm in a fix, but I'll work myself out of it again. Don't make things more diffi-cult for me than they already are. Speak up on my behalf in the office! People don't like traveling salesmen. I know that. People think they earn pots of money and thus lead a fine life. People don't even have any special reason to think through this judgment more clearly. But you, Mr. Manager, you have a better perspective on the interconnections than the other people, even, I tell you in total confidence, a better perspective than Mr. Chairman himself, who in his capacity as the employer may let his judgment make casual mistakes at the expense of an employee. You also know well enough that the traveling salesman who is outside the office almost the entire year can become so easily a victim of gossip, coincid-ences, and groundless complaints, against which it's im-possible for him to defend himself, since for the most part he doesn't hear about them at all and only then when he's ex-hausted after finishing a trip, and gets to feel in his own body at home the nasty consequences, which can't be thoroughly explored back to their origins. Mr. Manager, don't leave without speaking a word telling me that you'll at least concede that I'm a little in the right!"

But at Gregor's first words the manager had already turned away, and now he looked back at Gregor over his twitching shoulders with pursed lips. During Gregor's speech he was not still for a moment, but was moving away towards the door, without taking his eyes off Gregor, but really gradually, as if there was a secret ban on leaving the room. He was already in the hall, and after the sudden movement with which he finally pulled his foot out of the living room, one could have believed that he had just burned the sole of his foot. In the hall, however, he stretched out his right hand away from his body towards the staircase, as if some truly supernatural relief was waiting for him there.

Gregor realized that he must not under any circumstances allow the manager to go away in this frame of mind, especially if his position in the firm was not to be placed in the greatest danger. His parents did not understand all this very well. Over the long years, they had developed the conviction that Gregor was set up for life in his firm and, in addition, they had so much to do nowadays with their present troubles that all foresight was foreign to them. But Gregor had this foresight. The manager must be held back, calmed down, convinced, and finally won over. The future of Gregor and his family really depended on it! If only the sister had been there! She was clever. She had already cried while Gregor was still lying quietly on his back. And the manager, this friend of the ladies, would certainly let himself be guided by her. She would have closed the door to the apartment and talked him out of his fright in the hall. But the sister was not even there. Gregor must deal with it himself.

Without thinking that as yet he didn't know anything about his present ability to move and without thinking that his speech possibly (indeed probably) had once again not been understood, he left the wing of the door, pushed himself through the opening, and wanted to go over to the manager, who was already holding tight onto the handrail with both hands on the landing in a ridiculous way. But as he looked for something to hold onto, with a small scream Gregor immediately fell down onto his numerous little legs. Scarcely had this happened, when he felt for the first time that morning a general physical well being. The small limbs had firm floor under them; they obeyed perfectly, as he noticed to his joy, and strove to carry him forward in the direction he wanted. Right away he believed that the final amelioration of all his suffering was immediately at hand. But at the very moment when he lay on the floor rocking in a restrained manner quite close and directly across from his mother (apparently totally sunk into herself) she suddenly sprang right up with her arms spread far apart and her fingers extended and cried out, "Help, for God's sake, help!" She held her head bowed down, as if she wanted to view Gregor better, but ran senselessly back, contradicting that gesture, forgetting that behind her stood the table with all the dishes on it. When she reached the table, she sat down heavily on it, as if absent-mindedly, and did not appear to notice at all that next to her coffee was pouring out onto the carpet in a full stream from the large overturned container.

"Mother, mother," said Gregor quietly, and looked over towards her. The manager momentarily had disappeared completely from his mind; by contrast, at the sight of the flowing coffee he couldn't stop himself snapping his jaws in the air a few times . At that his mother screamed all over again, hurried from the table, and collapsed into the arms of his father, who was rushing towards her. But Gregor had no time right now for his parents: the manager was already on the staircase. His chin level with the banister, the manager looked back for the last time. Gregor took an initial movement to catch up to him if possible. But the manager must have suspected something, because he made a leap down over a few stairs and disappeared, still shouting "Huh!" The sound echoed throughout the entire stairwell.

Now, unfortunately this flight of the manager also seemed completely to bewilder his father, who earlier had been relatively calm, for instead of running after the manager himself or at least not hindering Gregor from his pursuit, with his right hand he grabbed hold of the manager's cane, which he had left behind with his hat and overcoat on a chair. With his left hand, his father picked up a large newspaper from the table and, stamping his feet on the floor, he set out to drive Gregor back into his room by waving the cane and the newspaper. No request of Gregor's was of any use; no request would even be understood. No matter how willing he was to turn his head respectfully, his father just stomped all the harder with his feet.

Across the room from him his mother had pulled open a window, in spite of the cool weather, and leaning out with her hands on her cheeks, she pushed her face far outside the window. Between the alley and the stair well a strong draught came up, the curtains on the window flew around, the newspapers on the table swished, and individual sheets fluttered down over the floor. The father relentlessly pressed forward pushing out sibilants, like a wild man. Now, Gregor had no practice at all in going backwards; it was really going very slowly. If Gregor only had been allowed to turn himself around, he would have been in his room right away, but he was afraid to make his father impatient by the time-consuming process of turning around, and each moment he faced the threat of a mortal blow on his back or his head from the cane in his father's hand. Finally Gregor had no other option, for he noticed with horror that he did not understand yet how to maintain his direction going backwards. And so he began, amid constantly anxious sideways glances in his father's direction, to turn himself around as quickly as possible (although in truth this was only very slowly). Perhaps his father noticed his good intentions, for he did not disrupt Gregor in this motion, but with the tip of the cane from a distance he even directed here and there Gregor's rotating movement.

If only there hadn't been his father's unbearable hissing! Because of that Gregor totally lost his head. He was already almost totally turned around, when, always with this hissing in his ear, he just made a mistake and turned himself back a little. But when he finally was successful in getting his head in front of the door opening, it became clear that his body was too wide to go through any further. Naturally his father, in his present mental state, had no idea of opening the other wing of the door a bit to create a suitable passage for Gregor to get through. His single fixed thought was that Gregor must get into his room as quickly as possible. He would never have allowed the elaborate preparations that Gregor required to orient himself and thus perhaps get through the door. On the contrary, as if there were no obstacle and with a peculiar noise, he now drove Gregor forwards. Behind Gregor the sound was at this point no longer like the voice of only a single father. Now it was really no longer a joke, and Gregor forced himself, come what might, into the door. One side of his body was lifted up. He lay at an angle in the door opening. His one flank was sore with the scraping. On the white door ugly blotches were left. Soon he was stuck fast and would have not been able to move any more on his own. The tiny legs on one side hung twitching in the air above, the ones on the other side were pushed painfully into the floor. Then his father gave him one really strong liberating push from behind, and he scurried, bleeding severely, far into the interior of his room. The door was slammed shut with the cane, and finally it was quiet.

II

Gregor first woke up from his heavy swoon-like sleep in the evening twilight. He would certainly have woken up soon afterwards without any disturbance, for he felt himself sufficiently rested and wide awake, although it appeared to him as if a hurried step and a cautious closing of the door to the hall had aroused him. The shine of the electric streetlights lay pale here and there on the ceiling and on the higher parts of the furniture, but underneath around Gregor it was dark. He pushed himself slowly toward the door, still groping awkwardly with his feelers, which he now learned to value for the first time, to check what was happening there. His left side seemed one single long unpleasantly stretched scar, and he really had to hobble on his two rows of legs. In addition, one small leg had been seriously wounded in the course of the morning incident (it was almost a miracle that only one had been hurt) and dragged lifelessly behind.

By the door he first noticed what had really lured him there: it was the smell of something to eat. For there stood a bowl filled with sweetened milk, in which swam tiny pieces of white bread. He almost laughed with joy, for he now had a much greater hunger than in the morning, and he immediately dipped his head almost up to and over his eyes down into the milk. But he soon drew it back again in disappointment, not just because it was difficult for him to eat on account of his delicate left side (he could eat only if his entire panting body worked in a coordinated way), but also because the milk, which otherwise was his favorite drink and which his sister had certainly placed there for that reason, did not appeal to him at all. He turned away from the bowl almost with aversion and crept back into the middle of the room.

In the living room, as Gregor saw through the crack in the door, the gas was lit, but where on other occasions at this time of day the father was accustomed to read the afternoon newspaper in a loud voice to his mother and sometimes also to his sister, at the moment not a sound was audible. Now, perhaps this reading aloud, about which his sister always spoken and written to him, had recently fallen out of their general routine. But it was so still all around, in spite of the fact that the apartment was certainly not empty. "What a quiet life the family leads", said Gregor to himself and, as he stared fixedly out in front of him into the darkness, he felt a great pride that he had been able to provide such a life in a beautiful apartment like this for his parents and his sister. But how would things go if now all tranquility, all prosperity, all contentment should come to a horrible end? In order not to lose himself in such thoughts, Gregor preferred to set himself moving and crawled up and down in his room.

Once during the long evening one side door and then the other door was opened just a tiny crack and quickly closed again. Someone presumably needed to come in but had then thought better of it. Gregor immediately took up a position by the living room door, determined to bring in the hesitant visitor somehow or other or at least to find out who it might be. But now the door was not opened any more, and Gregor waited in vain. Earlier, when the door had been barred, they had all wanted to come in to him; now, when he had opened one door and when the others had obviously been opened during the day, no one came any more, and the keys were stuck in the locks on the outside.

The light in the living room was turned off only late at night, and now it was easy to establish that his parents and his sister had stayed awake all this time, for one could hear clearly as all three moved away on tiptoe. Now it was certain that no one would come into Gregor any more until the morning. Thus, he had a long time to think undisturbed about how he should reorganize his life from scratch. But the high, open room, in which he was compelled to lie flat on the floor, made him anxious, without his being able to figure out the reason, for he had lived in the room for five years. With a half unconscious turn and not without a slight shame he scurried under the couch, where, in spite of the fact that his back was a little cramped and he could no longer lift up his head, he felt very comfortable and was sorry only that his body was too wide to fit completely under it.

There he remained the entire night, which he spent partly in a state of semi-sleep, out of which his hunger constantly woke him with a start, but partly in a state of worry and murky hopes, which all led to the conclusion that for the time being he would have to keep calm and with patience and the greatest consideration for his family tolerate the troubles which in his present condition he was now forced to cause them.

Already early in the morning (it was still almost night) Gregor had an opportunity to test the power of the decisions he had just made, for his sister, almost fully dressed, opened the door from the hall into his room and looked eagerly inside. She did not find him immediately, but when she noticed him under the couch (God, he had to be somewhere or other; for he could hardly fly away) she got such a shock that, without being able to control herself, she slammed the door shut once again from the outside. However, as if she was sorry for her behaviour, she immediately opened the door again and walked in on her tiptoes, as if she was in the presence of a serious invalid or a total stranger. Gregor had pushed his head forward just to the edge of the couch and was observing her. Would she really notice that he had left the milk standing, not indeed from any lack of hunger, and would she bring in something else to eat more suitable for him? If she did not do it on her own, he would sooner starve to death than call her attention to the fact, although he had a really powerful urge to move beyond the couch, throw himself at his sister's feet, and beg her for something or other good to eat. But his sister noticed right away with astonishment that the bowl was still full, with only a little milk spilled around it. She picked it up immediately (although not with her bare hands but with a rag), and took it out of the room. Gregor was extremely curious what she would bring as a substitute, and he pictured to himself different ideas about that. But he never could have guessed what his sister out of the goodness of her heart in fact did. She brought him, to test his taste, an entire selection, all spread out on an old newspaper.

There were old half-rotten vegetables, bones from the evening meal, covered with a white sauce which had almost solidified, some raisins and almonds, cheese, which Gregor had declared inedible two days earlier, a slice of dry bread, a slice of salted bread smeared with butter. In addition to all this, she put down a bowl (probably designated once and for all as Gregor's) into which she had poured some water. And out of her delicacy of feeling, since she knew that Gregor would not eat in front of her, she went away very quickly and even turned the key in the lock, so that Gregor could now observe that he could make himself as comfortable as he wished. Gregor's small limbs buzzed as the time for eating had come. His wounds must, in any case, have already healed completely. He felt no handicap on that score. He was astonished at that and thought about it, how more than a month ago he had cut his finger slightly with a knife and how this wound had hurt enough even the day before yesterday.

"Am I now going to be less sensitive," he thought, already sucking greedily on the cheese, which had strongly attracted him right away, more than all the other foods. Quickly and with his eyes watering with satisfaction, he ate one after the other the cheese, the vegetables, and the sauce; the fresh food, by contrast, didn't taste good to him. He couldn't bear the smell and even carried the things he wanted to eat a little distance away. By the time his sister slowly turned the key as a sign that he should withdraw, he was long finished and now lay lazily in the same spot. The noise immediately startled him, in spite of the fact that he was already almost asleep, and he scurried back again under the couch. But it cost him great self-control to remain under the couch, even for the short time his sister was in the room, because his body had filled out somewhat on account of the rich meal and in the narrow space there he could scarcely breathe. In the midst of minor attacks of asphyxiation, he looked at her with somewhat pro-truding eyes, as his unsuspecting sister swept up with a broom, not just the remnants, but even the foods which Gregor had not touched at all, as if these were also now use-less, and as she dumped everything quickly into a bucket, which she closed with a wooden lid, and then carried all of it out of the room. She had hardly turned around before Gregor had already dragged himself out from the couch, stretched out, and let his body expand.

In this way Gregor got his food every day, once in the morning, when his parents and the servant girl were still asleep, and a second time after the common noon meal, for his parents were, as before, asleep then for a little while, and the servant girl was sent off by his sister on some errand or other. Certainly they would not have wanted Gregor to starve to death, but perhaps they could not have endured finding out what he ate other than by hearsay. Perhaps his sister wanted to spare them what was possibly only a small grief, for they were really suffering quite enough already.

What sorts of excuses people had used on that first morn-ing to get the doctor and the locksmith out of the house Gregor was completely unable to ascertain. Since he was not comprehensible, no one, not even his sister, thought that he might be able to understand others, and thus, when his sister was in her room, he had to be content with listening now and then to her sighs and invocations to the saints. Only later, when she had grown somewhat accustomed to everything (naturally there could never be any talk of her growing completely accustomed to it) Gregor sometimes caught a comment which was intended to be friendly or could be interpreted as such. "Well, today it tasted good to him," she said, if Gregor had really cleaned up what he had to eat; whereas, in the reverse situation, which gradually repeated itself more and more frequently, she used to say sadly, "Now everything has stopped again."

But while Gregor could get no new information directly, he did hear a good deal from the room next door, and as soon as he heard voices, he scurried right away to the relevant door and pressed his entire body against it. In the early days especially, there was no conversation which was not concerned with him in some way or other, even if only in secret. For two days at all meal times discussions on that subject could be heard on how people should now behave; but they also talked about the same subject in the times between meals, for there were always at least two family members at home, since no one really wanted to remain in the house alone and people could not under any circumstances leave the apartment completely empty. In addition, on the very first day the servant girl (it was not completely clear what and how much she knew about what had happened) on her knees had begged his mother to let her go immediately, and when she said good bye about fifteen minutes later, she thanked them for the dismissal with tears in her eyes, as if she was receiving the greatest favour which people had shown her there, and, without anyone demanding it from her, she swore a fearful oath not to betray anyone, not even the slightest bit.

Now his sister had to team up with his mother to do the

cooking, although that didn't create much trouble because people were eating almost nothing. Again and again Gregor listened as one of them vainly invited another one to eat and received no answer other than "Thank you. I have enough" or something like that. And perhaps they had stopped having anything to drink, too. His sister often asked his father whether he wanted to have a beer and gladly offered to fetch it herself, and when his father was silent, she said, in order to remove any reservations he might have, that she could send the caretaker's wife to get it. But then his father finally said a resounding "No," and nothing more would be spoken about it.

Already during the first day his father laid out all the financial circumstances and prospects to his mother and to his sister as well. From time to time he stood up from the table and pulled out of the small lockbox salvaged from his business, which had collapsed five years previously, some document or other or some notebook. The sound was audible as he opened up the complicated lock and, after removing what he was looking for, locked it up again. These explanations by his father were, in part, the first enjoyable thing that Gregor had the chance to listen to since his imprisonment. He had thought that nothing at all was left over for his father from that business; at least his father had told him nothing to the contradict that view, and Gregor in any case hadn't asked him about it. At the time Gregor's only concern had been to devote everything he had in order to allow his family to forget as quickly as possible the business misfortune which had brought them all into a state of complete hopelessness. And so at that point he'd started to work with a special intensity and from an assistant had become, almost overnight, a traveling salesman, who naturally had entirely different possibilities for earning money and whose successes at work at once were converted into the form of cash commissions, which could be set out on the table at home in front of his astonished and delighted family. Those had been beautiful days, and they had never come back afterwards, at least not with the same splendour, in spite of the fact that Gregor later earned so much money that he was in a position to bear the expenses of the entire family, expenses which he, in fact, did bear. They had become quite accustomed to it, both the family and Gregor as well. They took the money with thanks, and he happily surrendered it, but the special warmth was no longer present. Only the sister had remained still close to Gregor, and it was his secret plan to send her (in contrast to Gregor she loved music very much and knew how to play the violin charmingly) next year to the conservatory, regardless of the great expense which that must necessitate and which would be made up in other ways. Now and then during Gregor's short stays in the city the conservatory was mentioned in conversations with his sister, but always only as a beautiful dream, whose realization was unimaginable, and their parents never listened to these innocent expectations with pleasure. But Gregor thought about them with scrupulous consideration and intended to explain the matter ceremoniously on Christmas Eve.

In his present situation, such futile ideas went through his head, while he pushed himself right up against the door and listened. Sometimes in his general exhaustion he couldn't listen any more and let his head bang listlessly against the door, but he immediately pulled himself together, for even the small sound which he made by this motion was heard near by and silenced everyone. " There he goes on again," said his father after a while, clearly turning towards the door, and only then would the interrupted conversation gradually be resumed again.

Gregor found out clearly enough (for his father tended to repeat himself often in his explanations, partly because he had not personally concerned himself with these matters for a long time now, and partly also because his mother did not understand everything right away the first time) that, in spite all bad luck, a fortune, although a very small one, was available from the old times, which the interest (which had not been touched) had in the intervening time gradually allowed to increase a little. Furthermore, in addition to this, the money which Gregor had brought home every month (he had kept only a few florins for himself) had not been completely spent and had grown into a small capital amount. Gregor, behind his door, nodded eagerly, rejoicing over this unanticipated foresight and frugality. True, with this excess money, he could have paid off more of his father's debt to his employer and the day on which he could be rid of this position would have been a lot closer, but now things were doubtless better the way his father had arranged them.

At the moment, however, this money was nowhere near sufficient to permit the family to live on the interest payments. Perhaps it would be enough to maintain the family for one or at most two years, that's all. Thus it came only to an amount which one should not really take out and which must be set aside for an emergency. But the money to live on must be earned. Now, his father was a healthy man, although he was old, who had not worked at all for five years now and thus could not be counted on for very much. He had in these five years, the first holidays of his trouble-filled but unsuccessful life, put on a good deal of fat and thus had become really heavy. And should his old mother now maybe work for money, a woman who suffered from asthma, for whom wandering through the apartment even now was a great strain and who spent every second day on the sofa by the open window labouring for breath? Should his sister earn money, a girl who was still a seventeen-year-old child, whose earlier life style had been so very delightful that it had consisted of dressing herself nicely, sleeping in late, helping around the house, taking part in a few modest enjoyments and, above all, playing the violin? When it came to talking about this need to earn money, at first Gregor went away from the door and threw himself on the cool leather sofa beside the door, for he was quite hot from shame and sorrow.

Often he lay there all night long. He didn't sleep a moment and just scratched on the leather for hours at a time. He undertook the very difficult task of shoving a chair over to the window. Then he crept up on the window sill and, braced in the chair, leaned against the window to look out, obviously with some memory or other of the satisfaction which that used to bring him in earlier times. Actually from day to day he perceived things with less and less clarity, even those a short distance away: the hospital across the street, the all too frequent sight of which he had previously cursed, was not visible at all any more, and if he had not been precisely aware that he lived in the quiet but completely urban Charlotte Street, he could have believed that from his window he was peering out at a featureless wasteland, in which the gray heaven and the gray earth had merged and were indistinguishable. His attentive sister must have observed a couple of times that the chair stood by the window; then, after cleaning up the room, each time she pushed the chair back right against the window and from now on she even left the inner casement open.

If Gregor had only been able to speak to his sister and thank her for everything that she had to do for him, he would have tolerated her service more easily. As it was he suffered under it. The sister admittedly sought to cover up the awkwardness of everything as much as possible, and, as time went by, she naturally got more successful at it. But with the passing of time Gregor also came to understand everything more precisely. Even her entrance was terrible for him. As soon as she entered, she ran straight to the window, without taking the time to shut the door (in spite of the fact that she was otherwise very considerate in sparing anyone the sight of Gregor's room), and yanked the window open with eager hands, as if she was almost suffocating, and remained for a while by the window breathing deeply, even when it was still so cold. With this running and noise she frightened Gregor twice every day. The entire time he trembled under the couch, and yet he knew very well that she would certainly have spared him gladly if it had only been possible to remain with the window closed in a room where Gregor lived.

On one occasion (about one month had already gone by since Gregor's transformation, and there was now no particular reason any more for his sister to be startled at Gregor's appearance) she came a little earlier than usual and came upon

Gregor as he was still looking out the window, immobile and well positioned to frighten someone. It would not have come as a surprise to Gregor if she had not come in, since his position was preventing her from opening the window immediately. But she not only did not step inside; she even retreated and shut the door. A stranger really could have concluded from this that Gregor had been lying in wait for her and wanted to bite her. Of course, Gregor immediately concealed himself under the couch, but he had to wait until the noon meal before his sister returned, and she seemed much less calm than usual. From this he realized that his appearance was still constantly intolerable to her and must remain intolerable in future, and that she really had to exert a lot of self-control not to run away from a glimpse of only the small part of his body which stuck out from under the couch. In order to spare her even this sight, one day he dragged the sheet on his back onto the couch (this task took him four hours) and arranged it in such a way that he was now completely concealed and his sister, even if she bent down, could not see him. If this sheet was not necessary as far as she was concerned, then she could remove it, for it was clear enough that Gregor could not derive any pleasure from isolating himself away so completely. But she left the sheet just as it was, and Gregor believed he even caught a look of gratitude when on one occasion he carefully lifted up the sheet a little with his head to check as his sister took stock of the new arrangement.

In the first two weeks his parents could not bring themselves to visit him, and he often heard how they fully acknowledged his sister's present work; whereas, earlier they had often got annoyed at his sister because she had seemed to them a somewhat useless young woman. However, now both his father and his mother often waited in front of Gregor's door while his sister cleaned up inside, and as soon as she came out she had to explain in detail how things looked in the room, what Gregor had eaten, how he had behaved this time, and whether perhaps a slight improvement was perceptible. In any event, his mother comparatively soon wanted to visit Gregor, but his father and his sister restrained her, at first with reasons which Gregor listened to very attentively and which he completely endorsed. Later, however, they had to hold her back forcefully, and when she then cried "Let me go to Gregor. He's my unlucky son! Don't you understand that I have to go to him?" Gregor then thought that perhaps it would be a good thing if his mother came in, not every day, of course, but maybe once a week. She understood everything much better than his sister, who in spite of all her courage was still a child and, in the last analysis, had perhaps undertaken such a difficult task only out of childish recklessness.

Gregor's wish to see his mother was soon realized. While during the day Gregor, out of consideration for his parents, did not want to show himself by the window, he couldn't crawl around very much on the few square metres of the floor. He found it difficult to bear lying quietly during the night, and soon eating no longer gave him the slightest pleasure. So for diversion he acquired the habit of crawling back and forth across the walls and ceiling. He was especially fond of hanging from the ceiling. The experience was quite different from lying on the floor. It was easier to breathe, a slight vibration went through his body, and in the midst of the almost happy amusement which Gregor found up there, it could happen that, to his own surprise, he let go and hit the floor. However, now he naturally controlled his body quite differently, and he did not injure himself in such a great fall. His sister noticed immediately the new amusement which Gregor had found for himself (for as he crept around he left behind here and there traces of his sticky stuff), and so she got the idea of making Gregor's creeping around as easy as possible and thus of removing the furniture which got in the way, especially the chest of drawers and the writing desk.

But she was in no position to do this by herself. She did not dare to ask her father to help, and the servant girl would certainly not have assisted her, for although this girl, about sixteen years old, had courageously remained since the dismissal of the previous cook, she had begged for the privilege of being allowed to stay permanently confined to the kitchen and of having to open the door only in answer to a special summons. Thus, his sister had no other choice but to involve his mother while his father was absent. His mother approached Gregor's room with cries of excited joy, but she fell silent at the door. Of course, his sister first checked whether everything in the room was in order. Only then did she let his mother walk in. In great haste Gregor had drawn the sheet down even further and wrinkled it more. The whole thing really looked just like a coverlet thrown carelessly over the couch. On this occasion, Gregor held back from spying out from under the sheet. Thus, he refrained from looking at his mother this time and was just happy that she had come. "Come on; he is not visible," said his sister, and evidently led his mother by the hand. Now Gregor listened as these two weak women shifted the still heavy old chest of drawers from its position, and as his sister constantly took on herself the greatest part of the work, without listening to the warnings of his mother who was afraid that she would strain herself. The work lasted a long time. After about a quarter of an hour had already gone by his mother said that it would be better if they left the chest of drawers where it was, because, in the first place, it was too heavy: they would not be finished before his father's arrival, and with the chest of drawers in the middle of the room it would block all Gregor's pathways, but, in the second place, it might not be certain that Gregor would be pleased with the removal of the furniture. To her the reverse seemed to be true; the sight of the empty walls pierced her right to the heart, and why should Gregor not feel the same, since he had been accustomed to the room furnishings for a long time and in an empty room would thus feel himself abandoned.

"And is it not the case," his mother concluded very quietly, almost whispering as if she wished to prevent Gregor, whose exact location she really didn't know, from hearing even the sound of her voice (for she was convinced that he did not understand her words), "and isn't it a fact that by removing the furniture we're showing that we're giving up all hope of an improvement and are leaving him to his own resources without any consideration? I think it would be best if we tried to keep the room exactly in the condition in which it was before, so that, when Gregor returns to us, he finds everything unchanged and can forget the intervening time all the more easily."

As he heard his mother's words Gregor realized that the

lack of all immediate human contact, together with the monotonous life surrounded by the family over the course of these two months must have confused his understanding, because otherwise he couldn't explain to himself that he in all seriousness could've been so keen to have his room emptied. Was he really eager to let the warm room, comfortably furnished with pieces he had inherited, be turned into a cavern in which he would, of course, then be able to crawl about in all directions without disturbance, but at the same time with a quick and complete forgetting of his human past as well? Was he then at this point already on the verge of forgetting and was it only the voice of his mother, which he had not heard for along time, that had aroused him? Nothing was to be removed; everything must remain. In his condition he couldn't function without the beneficial influences of his furniture. And if the furniture prevented him from carrying out his senseless crawling about all over the place, then there was no harm in that, but rather a great benefit.

But his sister unfortunately thought otherwise. She had grown accustomed, certainly not without justification, so far as the discussion of matters concerning Gregor was concerned, to act as an special expert with respect to their parents, and so now the mother's advice was for his sister sufficient reason to insist on the removal, not only of the chest of drawers and the writing desk, which were the only items she had thought about at first, but also of all the furniture, with the exception of the indispensable couch. Of course, it was not only childish defiance and her recent very unexpected and hard won self-confidence which led her to this demand. She had also actually observed that Gregor needed a great deal of room to creep about; the furniture, on the other hand, as far as one could see, was not of the slightest use.

But perhaps the enthusiastic sensibility of young women of her age also played a role. This feeling sought release at every opportunity, and with it Grete now felt tempted to want to make Gregor's situation even more terrifying, so that then she would be able to do even more for him than now. For surely no one except Grete would ever trust themselves to enter a room in which Gregor ruled the empty walls all by himself. And so she did not let herself be dissuaded from her decision by her mother, who in this room seemed uncertain of herself in her sheer agitation and soon kept quiet, helping his sister with all her energy to get the chest of drawers out of the room. Now, Gregor could still do without the chest of drawers if need be, but the writing desk really had to stay. And scarcely had the women left the room with the chest of drawers, groaning as they pushed it, when Gregor stuck his head out from under the sofa to take a look how he could intervene cautiously and with as much consideration as possible. But unfortunately it was his mother who came back into the room first, while Grete had her arms wrapped around the chest of drawers in the next room and was rocking it back and forth by herself, without moving it from its position. His mother was not used to the sight of Gregor; he could have made her ill, and so, frightened, Gregor scurried backwards right to the other end of the sofa, but he could no longer prevent the sheet from moving forward a little. That was enough to catch his mother's attention. She came to a halt, stood still for a moment, and then went back to Grete.

Although Gregor kept repeating to himself over and over

that really nothing unusual was going on, that only a few pieces of furniture were being rearranged, he soon had to admit to himself that the movements of the women to and fro, their quiet conversations, the scratching of the furniture on the floor affected him like a great swollen commotion on all sides, and, so firmly was he pulling in his head and legs and pressing his body into the floor, he had to tell himself unequivocally that he wouldn't be able to endure all this much longer. They were cleaning out his room, taking away from him everything he cherished; they had already dragged out the chest of drawers in which the fret saw and other tools were kept, and they were now loosening the writing desk which was fixed tight to the floor, the desk on which he, as a business student, a school student, indeed even as an elementary school student, had written out his assignments. At that moment he really didn't have any more time to check the good intentions of the two women, whose existence he had in any case almost forgotten, because in their exhaustion they were working really silently, and the heavy stumbling of their feet was the only sound to be heard.

And so he scuttled out (the women were just propping themselves up on the writing desk in the next room in order to take a breather) changing the direction of his path four times. He really didn't know what he should rescue first. Then he saw hanging conspicuously on the wall, which was otherwise already empty, the picture of the woman dressed in nothing but fur. He quickly scurried up over it and pressed himself against the glass that held it in place and which made his hot abdomen feel good. At least this picture, which Gregor at the moment completely concealed, surely no one would now take away. He twisted his head towards the door of the living room to observe the women as they came back in.

They had not allowed themselves very much rest and were coming back right away. Grete had placed her arm around her mother and held her tightly. "So what shall we take now?" said Grete and looked around her. Then her glance crossed with Gregor's from the wall. She kept her composure only because her mother was there. She bent her face towards her mother in order to prevent her from looking around, and said, although in a trembling voice and too quickly, "Come, wouldn't it be better to go back to the living room for just another moment?" Grete's purpose was clear to Gregor: she wanted to bring his mother to a safe place and then chase him down from the wall. Well, let her just attempt that! He squatted on his picture and did not hand it over. He would sooner spring into Grete's face.

But Grete's words had immediately made the mother very uneasy. She walked to the side, caught sight of the enormous brown splotch on the flowered wallpaper, and, before she became truly aware that what she was looking at was Gregor, screamed out in a high pitched raw voice "Oh God, oh God" and fell with outstretched arms, as if she was surrendering everything, down onto the couch and lay there motionless. "Gregor, you. . .," cried out his sister with a raised fist and an urgent glare. Since his transformation those were the first words which she had directed right at him. She ran into the room next door to bring some spirits or other with which she could revive her mother from her fainting spell. Gregor wanted to help as well (there was time enough to save the picture), but he was stuck fast on the glass and had to tear himself loose forcefully. Then he also scurried into the next room, as if he could give his sister some advice, as in earlier times, but then he had to stand there idly behind her, while she rummaged about among various small bottles. Still, she was frightened when she turned around. A bottle fell onto the floor and shattered. A splinter of glass wounded Gregor in the face, some corrosive medicine or other dripped over him. Now, without lingering any longer, Grete took as many small bottles as she could hold and ran with them into her mother. She slammed the door shut with her foot. Gregor was now shut off from his mother, who was perhaps near death, thanks to him. He could not open the door, and he did not want to chase away his sister who had to remain with her mother. At this point he had nothing to do but wait, and overwhelmed with self-reproach and worry, he began to creep and crawl over everything: walls, furniture, and ceiling,. Finally, in his despair, as the entire room started to spin around him, he fell onto the middle of the large table.

A short time elapsed. Gregor lay there limply. All around was still. Perhaps that was a good sign. Then there was ring at the door. The servant girl was naturally shut up in her kit- chen, and Grete must therefore go to open the door. The father had arrived. "What's happened," were his first words. Grete's appearance had told him everything. Grete replied with a dull voice; evidently she was pressing her face into her father's chest: "Mother fainted, but she's getting better now. Gregor has broken loose." "Yes, I have expected that," said his father, "I always told you that, but you women don't want to listen."

It was clear to Gregor that his father had badly misunderstood Grete's short message and was assuming that Gregor had committed some violent crime or other. Thus, Gregor now had to find his father to calm him down, for he had neither the time nor the opportunity to clarify things for him. And so he rushed away to the door of his room and pushed himself against it, so that his father could see right away as he entered from the hall that Gregor fully intended to return at once to his room, that it was not necessary to drive him back, but that one only needed to open the door and he would disappear immediately.

But his father was not in the mood to observe such niceties. "Ah," he yelled as soon as he entered, with a tone as if he were all at once angry and pleased. Gregor pulled his head back from the door and raised it in the direction of his father. He had not really pictured his father as he now stood there. Of course, what with his new style of creeping all around, he had in the past while neglected to pay attention to what was going on in the rest of the apartment, as he had done before, and really should have grasped the fact that he would encounter different conditions. Nevertheless, nevertheless, was that still his father? Was that the same man who had lain exhausted and buried in bed in earlier days when Gregor was setting out on a business trip, who had received him on the evenings of his return in a sleeping gown and arm chair, totally incapable of standing up, who had only lifted his arm as a sign of happiness, and who in their rare strolls together a few Sundays a year and on the important holidays made his way slowly forwards between Gregor and his mother (who themselves moved slowly), always a bit more slowly than them, bundled up in his old coat, all the time setting down his walking stick carefully, and who, when he had wanted to say something, almost always stood still and gathered his entourage around him?

But now he was standing up really straight, dressed in a tight fitting blue uniform with gold buttons, like the ones servants wear in a banking company. Above the high stiff collar of his jacket his firm double chin stuck out prominently, beneath his bushy eyebrows the glance of his black eyes was freshly penetrating and alert, his otherwise disheveled white hair was combed down into a carefully exact shining part. He threw his cap, on which a gold monogram (apparently the symbol of the bank) was affixed, in an arc across the entire room onto the sofa and moved, throwing back the edge of the long coat of his uniform, with his hands in his trouser pockets and a grim face, right up to Gregor.

He really didn't know what he had in mind, but he raised his foot uncommonly high anyway, and Gregor was astonished at the gigantic size of his sole of his boot. However, he did not linger on that point. For he knew from the first day of his new life that as far as he was concerned his father considered the greatest force the only appropriate response. And so he scurried away from his father, stopped when his father remained standing, and scampered forward again when his father merely stirred. In this way they made their way around the room repeatedly, without anything decisive taking place; indeed because of the slow pace it didn't look like a chase. Gregor remained on the floor for the time being, especially as he was afraid that his father could take a flight up onto the wall or the ceiling as an act of real malice. At any event

Gregor had to tell himself that he couldn't keep up this running around for a long time, because whenever his father took a single step, he had to go through an enormous number of movements. Already he was starting to suffer from a shortage of breath, just as in his earlier days his lungs had been quite unreliable. As he now staggered around in this way in order to gather all his energies for running, hardly keeping his eyes open, in his listlessness he had no notion at all of any escape other than by running and had almost already forgotten that the walls were available to him, although they were obstructed by carefully carved furniture full of sharp points and spikes--at that moment something or other thrown casually flew down close by and rolled in front of him. It was an apple; immediately a second one flew after it. Gregor stood still in fright. Further flight was useless, for his father had decided to bombard him.

From the fruit bowl on the sideboard his father had filled his pockets, and now, without for the moment taking accurate aim, was throwing apple after apple. These small red apples rolled as if electrified around on the floor and collided with each other. A weakly thrown apple grazed Gregor's back but skidded off harmlessly. However another thrown immediately after that one drove into Gregor's back really hard. Gregor wanted to drag himself off, as if the unexpected and incredible pain would go away if he changed his position. But he felt as if he was nailed in place and lay stretched out completely confused in all his senses. Only with his final glance did he notice how the door of his room was pulled open and how, right in front of his sister (who was yelling), his mother ran out in her undergarments, for his sister had undressed her in order to give her some freedom to breathe in her fainting spell, and how his mother then ran up to his father, on the way her tied up skirts one after the other slipped toward the floor, and how, tripping over her skirts, she hurled herself onto his father and, throwing her arms around him, in complete union with him--but at this moment Gregor's powers of sight gave way--as her hands reached to the back of his father's head and she begged him to spare Gregor's life.

III

Gregor's serious wound, from which he suffered for over a month (since no one ventured to remove the apple, it remained in his flesh as a visible reminder), seemed by itself to have reminded the father that, in spite of his present unhappy and hateful appearance, Gregor was a member of the family, something one should not treat as an enemy, and that it was, on the contrary, a requirement of family duty to suppress one's aversion and to endure--nothing else, just endure. And if through his wound Gregor had now apparently lost for good his ability to move and for the time being needed many many minutes to crawl across this room, like an aged invalid (so far as creeping up high was concerned, that was unimaginable), nevertheless for this worsening of his condition, in his opinion, he did get completely satisfactory compensation, because every day towards evening the door to the living room, which he was in the habit of keeping a sharp eye on even one or two hours beforehand, was opened, so that he, lying down in the darkness of his room, invisible from the living room, could see the entire family at the illuminated table and listen to their conversation, to a certain extent with their common permission, a situation quite different from what happened before.

Of course, it was no longer the animated social interaction of former times, about which Gregor in small hotel rooms had always thought about with a certain longing, when, tired out, he had to throw himself in the damp bedclothes. For the most part what went on now was very quiet. After the evening meal the father fell asleep quickly in his arm chair; the mother and sister talked guardedly to each other in the stillness. Bent far over, the mother sewed fine undergarments for a fashion shop. The sister, who had taken on a job as a salesgirl, in the evening studied stenography and French, so as perhaps later to obtain a better position. Sometimes the father woke up and, as if he was quite ignorant that he had been asleep, said to the mother "How long you have been sewing today!" and went right back to sleep, while the mother and the sister smiled tiredly to each other.

With a sort of stubbornness the father refused to take off his servant's uniform even at home, and while his sleeping gown hung unused on the coat hook, the father dozed completely dressed in his place, as if he was always ready for his responsibility and even here was waiting for the voice of his superior. As result, in spite of all the care of the mother and sister, his uniform, which even at the start was not new, grew dirty, and Gregor looked, often for the entire evening, at this clothing, with stains all over it and with its gold buttons always polished, in which the old man, although very uncomfortable, slept peacefully nonetheless.

As soon as the clock struck ten, the mother tried encouraging the father gently to wake up and then persuading him to go to bed, on the ground that he couldn't get a proper sleep here and the father, who had to report for service at six o'clock, really needed a good sleep. But in his stubbornness, which had gripped him since he had become a servant, he insisted always on staying even longer by the table, although he regularly fell asleep and then could only be prevailed upon with the greatest difficulty to trade his chair for the bed. No matter how much the mother and sister might at that point work on him with small admonitions, for a quarter of an hour he would remain shaking his head slowly, his eyes closed, without standing up. The mother would pull him by the sleeve and speak flattering words into his ear; the sister would leave her work to help her mother, but that would not have the desired effect on the father. He would settle himself even more deeply in his arm chair. Only when the two women grabbed him under the armpits would he throw his eyes open, look back and forth at the mother and sister, and habitually say "This is a life. This is the peace and quiet of my old age." And propped up by both women, he would heave himself up, elaborately, as if for him it was the greatest travail, allow himself to be led to the door by the women, wave them away there, and proceed on his own from there, while the mother quickly threw down her sewing implements and the sister her pen in order to run after the father and help him some more.

In this overworked and exhausted family who had time to worry any longer about Gregor more than was absolutely necessary? The household was constantly getting smaller. The servant girl was now let go. A huge bony cleaning woman with white hair flapping all over her head came in the morning and the evening to do the heaviest work. The mother took care of everything else in addition to her considerable sewing work. It even happened that various pieces of family jewelry, which previously the mother and sister had been overjoyed to wear on social and festive occasions, were sold, as Gregor found out in the evening from the general discussion of the prices they had fetched. But the greatest complaint was always that they could not leave this apartment, which was too big for their present means, since it was impossible to imagine how Gregor might be moved. But Gregor fully recognized that it was not just consideration for him which was preventing a move (for he could have been transported easily in a suitable box with a few air holes); the main thing holding the family back from a change in living quarters was far more their complete hopelessness and the idea that they had been struck by a misfortune like no one else in their entire circle of relatives and acquaintances.

What the world demands of poor people they now carried out to an extreme degree. The father brought breakfast to the petty officials at the bank, the mother sacrificed herself for the undergarments of strangers, the sister behind her desk was at the beck and call of customers, but the family's energies did not extend any further. And the wound in his back began to pain Gregor all over again, when now mother and sister, after they had escorted the father to bed, came back, let their work lie, moved close together, and sat cheek to cheek and when his mother would now say, pointing to Gregor's room, "Close the door, Grete," and when Gregor was again in the darkness, while close by the women mingled their tears or, quite dry eyed, stared at the table.

Gregor spent his nights and days with hardly any sleep.

Sometimes he thought that the next time the door opened he would take over the family arrangements just as he had earlier. In his imagination appeared again, after a long time, his employer and supervisor and the apprentices, the excessively gormless custodian, two or three friends from other businesses, a chambermaid from a hotel in the provinces, a loving fleeting memory, a female cashier from a hat shop, whom he had seriously, but too slowly courted--they all appeared mixed in with strangers or people he had already forgotten, but instead of helping him and his family, they were all unapproachable, and he was happy to see them disappear.

But then he was in no mood to worry about his family. He was filled with sheer anger over the wretched care he was getting, even though he couldn't imagine anything for which he might have an appetite. Still, he made plans about how he could take from the larder what he at all account deserved, even if he wasn't hungry. Without thinking any more about how one might be able to give Gregor special pleasure, the sister now kicked some food or other very quickly into his room in the morning and at noon, before she ran off to her shop, and in the evening, quite indifferent about whether the food had perhaps only been tasted or, what happened most frequently, remained entirely undisturbed, she whisked it out with one sweep of her broom. The task of cleaning his room, which she now always carried out in the evening, could not be done any more quickly. Streaks of dirt ran along the walls; here and there lay tangles of dust and garbage. At first, when his sister arrived, Gregor positioned himself in a particularly filthy corner in order with this posture to make something of a protest. But he could have well stayed there for weeks without his sister's changing her ways. Indeed, she perceived the dirt as much as he did, but she had decided just to let it stay.

In this business, with a touchiness which was quite new to her and which had generally taken over the entire family, she kept watch to see that the cleaning of Gregor's room remained reserved for her. Once his mother had undertaken a major cleaning of Gregor's room, which she had only completed successfully after using a few buckets of water. But the extensive dampness made Gregor sick and he lay supine, embittered and immobile on the couch. However, the mother's punishment was not delayed for long. For in the evening the sister had hardly observed the change in Gregor's room before she ran into the living room mightily offended and, in spite of her mother's hand lifted high in entreaty, broke out in a fit of crying. Her parents (the father had, of course, woken up with a start in his arm chair) at first looked at her astonished and helpless; until they started to get agitated. Turning to his right, the father heaped reproaches on the mother that she was not to take over the cleaning of Gregor's room from the sister and, turning to his left, he shouted at the sister that she would no longer be allowed to clean Gregor's room ever again, while the mother tried to pull the father, beside himself in his excitement, into the bed room; the sister, shaken by her crying fit, pounded on the table with her tiny fists, and Gregor hissed at all this, angry that no one thought about shutting the door and sparing him the sight of this commotion.

But even when the sister, exhausted from her daily work, had grown tired of caring for Gregor as she had before, even then the mother did not have to come at all on her behalf. And Gregor did not have to be neglected. For now the cleaning woman was there. This old widow, who in her long life must have managed to survive the worst with the help of her bony frame, had no real horror of Gregor. Without being in the least curious, she had once by chance opened Gregor's door. At the sight of Gregor, who, totally surprised, began to scamper here and there, although no one was chasing him, she remained standing with her hands folded across her stomach staring at him. Since then she did not fail to open the door furtively a little every morning and evening to look in on Gregor. At first, she also called him to her with words which she presumably thought were friendly, like "Come here for a bit, old dung beetle!" or "Hey, look at the old dung beetle!" Addressed in such a manner, Gregor answered nothing, but remained motionless in his place, as if the door had not been opened at all. If only, instead of allowing this cleaning woman to disturb him uselessly whenever she felt like it, they had instead given her orders to clean up his room every day! One day in the early morning (a hard downpour, perhaps already a sign of the coming spring, struck the window panes) when the cleaning woman started up once again with her usual conversation, Gregor was so bitter that he turned towards her, as if for an attack, although slowly and weakly. But instead of being afraid of him, the cleaning woman merely lifted up a chair standing close by the door and, as she stood there with her mouth wide open, her intention was clear: she would close her mouth only when the chair in her hand had been thrown down on Gregor's back. "This goes no further, all right?" she asked, as Gregor turned himself around again, and she placed the chair calmly back in the corner.

Gregor ate hardly anything any more. Only when he chanced to move past the food which had been prepared did he, as a game, take a bit into his mouth, hold it there for hours, and generally spit it out again. At first he thought it might be his sadness over the condition of his room which kept him from eating, but he very soon became reconciled to the alterations in his room. People had grown accustomed to put into storage in his room things which they couldn't put anywhere else, and at this point there were many such things, now that they had rented one room of the apartment to three lodgers. These solemn gentlemen (all three had full beards, as Gregor once found out through a crack in the door) were meticulously intent on tidiness, not only in their own room but (since they had now rented a room here) in the entire household, and particularly in the kitchen. They simply did not tolerate any useless or shoddy stuff. Moreover, for the most part they had brought with them their own pieces of furniture. Thus, many items had become superfluous, and these were not really things one could sell or things people wanted to throw out. All these items ended up in Gregor's room, even the box of ashes and the garbage pail from the kitchen. The cleaning woman, always in a hurry, simply flung anything that was momentarily useless into Gregor's room. Fortunately Gregor generally saw only the relevant object and the hand which held it. The cleaning woman perhaps was intending, when time and opportunity allowed, to take the stuff out again or to throw everything out all at once, but in fact the things remained lying there, wherever they had ended up at the first throw, unless Gregor squirmed his way through the accumulation of junk and moved it. At first he was forced to do this because otherwise there was no room for him to creep around, but later he did it with a with a growing pleasure, although after such movements, tired to death and feeling wretched, he didn't budge for hours.

Because the lodgers sometimes also took their evening meal at home in the common living room, the door to the living room stayed shut on many evenings. But Gregor had no trouble at all going without the open door. Already on many evenings when it was open he had not availed himself of it, but, without the family noticing, was stretched out in the darkest corner of his room. However, once the cleaning woman had left the door to the living room slightly ajar, and it remained open even when the lodgers came in in the evening and the lights were put on. They sat down at the head of the table, where in earlier days the mother, the father, and Gregor had eaten, unfolded their serviettes, and picked up their knives and forks. The mother immediately appeared in the door with a dish of meat and right behind her the sister with a dish piled high with potatoes. The food gave off a lot of steam. The gentlemen lodgers bent over the plate set before them, as if they wanted to check it before eating, and in fact the one who sat in the middle (for the other two he seemed to serve as the authority) cut off a piece of meat still on the plate obviously to establish whether it was sufficiently tender and whether or not something should be shipped back to the kitchen. He was satisfied, and mother and sister, who had looked on in suspense, began to breathe easily and to smile.

The family itself ate in the kitchen. In spite of that, before the father went into the kitchen, he came into the room and with a single bow, cap in hand, made a tour of the table. The lodgers rose up collectively and murmured something in their beards. Then, when they were alone, they ate almost in complete silence. It seemed odd to Gregor that out of all the many different sorts of sounds of eating, what was always audible was their chewing teeth, as if by that Gregor should be shown that people needed their teeth to eat and that nothing could be done even with the most handsome toothless jawbone. "I really do have an appetite," Gregor said to himself sorrowfully, "but not for these things. How these lodgers stuff themselves, and I am dying."

On this very evening (Gregor didn't remember hearing the violin all through this period) it sounded from the kitchen. The lodgers had already ended their night meal, the middle one had pulled out a newspaper and had given each of the other two a page, and they were now leaning back, reading and smoking. When the violin started playing, they became attentive, got up, and went on tiptoe to the hall door, at which they remained standing pressed up against one another. They must have been audible from the kitchen, because the father called out "Perhaps the gentlemen don't like the playing? It can be stopped at once." "On the contrary," stated the lodger in the middle, "might the young woman not come into us and play in the room here where it is really much more comfortable and cheerful?" "Oh, thank you," cried out the father, as if he were the one playing the violin. The men stepped back into the room and waited. Soon the father came with the music stand, the mother with the sheet music, and the sister with the violin. The sister calmly prepared everything for the recital. The parents, who had never previously rented a room and therefore exaggerated their politeness to the lodgers, dared not sit on their own chairs. The father leaned against the door, his right hand stuck between two buttons of his buttoned up uniform. The mother, however, accepted a chair offered by one lodger. Since she left the chair sit where the gentleman had chanced to put it, she sat to one side in a corner.

The sister began to play. The father and mother, followed attentively, one on each side, the movements of her hands. Attracted by the playing, Gregor had ventured to advance a little further forward and his head was already in the living room. He scarcely wondered about the fact that recently he had had so little consideration for the others; earlier this consideration had been something he was proud of. And for that very reason he would've had at this moment more reason to hide away, because as a result of the dust which lay all over his room and flew around with the slightest movement, he was totally covered in dirt. On his back and his sides he carted around with him dust, threads, hair, and remnants of food. His indifference to everything was much too great for him to lie on his back and scour himself on the carpet, as he often had done earlier during the day. In spite of his condition he had no timidity about inching forward a bit on the spotless floor of the living room.

In any case, no one paid him any attention. The family was all caught up in the violin playing. The lodgers, by contrast, who for the moment had placed themselves, their hands in their trouser pockets, behind the music stand much too close to the sister, so that they could all see the sheet music, something that must certainly bother the sister, soon drew back to the window conversing in low voices with bowed heads, where they then remained, worriedly observed by the father. It now seemed really clear that, having assumed they were to hear a beautiful or entertaining violin recital, they were disappointed, and were allowing their peace and quiet to be disturbed only out of politeness. The way in which they all blew the smoke from their cigars out of their noses and mouths in particular led one to conclude that they were very irritated. And yet his sister was playing so beautifully. Her face was turned to the side, her gaze followed the score intently and sadly. Gregor crept forward still a little further and kept his head close against the floor in order to be able to catch her gaze if possible. Was he an animal that music so seized him? For him it was as if the way to the unknown nourishment he craved was revealing itself to him. He was determined to press forward right to his sister, to tug at her dress and to indicate to her in this way that she might still come with her violin into his room, because here no one valued the recital as he wanted to value it. He did not wish to let her go from his room any more, at least not as long as he lived. His frightening appearance would for the first time become useful for him. He wanted to be at all the doors of his room simultaneously and snarl back at the attackers. However, his sister should not be compelled but would remain with him voluntarily; she would sit next to him on the sofa, bend down her ear to him, and he would then confide in her that he firmly intended to send her to the conservatory and that, if his misfortune had not arrived in the interim, he would have declared all this last Christmas (had Christmas really already come and gone?), and would have brooked no argument. After this explanation his sister would break out in tears of emotion, and Gregor would lift himself up to her armpit and kiss her throat, which she, from the time she started going to work, had left exposed without a band or a collar.

"Mr. Samsa," called out the middle lodger to the father, and pointed his index finger, without uttering a further word, at Gregor as he was moving slowly forward. The violin fell silent. The middle lodger smiled, first shaking his head once at his friends, and then looked down at Gregor once more. Rather than driving Gregor back again, the father seemed to consider it of prime importance to calm down the lodgers, although they were not at all upset and Gregor seemed to entertain them more than the violin recital. The father hurried over to them and with outstretched arms tried to push them into their own room and simultaneously to block their view of Gregor with his own body. At this point they became really somewhat irritated, although one no longer knew whether that was because of the father's behaviour or because of knowledge they had just acquired that they had had, without knowing it, a neighbour like Gregor. They demanded explanations from his father, raised their arms to make their points, tugged agitatedly at their beards, and moved back towards their room quite slowly. In the meantime, the isolation which had suddenly fallen upon his sister after the sudden breaking off of the recital had overwhelmed her. She had held onto the violin and bow in her limp hands for a little while and had continued to look at the sheet music as if she was still playing. All at once she pulled herself together, placed the instrument in her mother's lap (the mother was still sitting in

her chair having trouble breathing and with her lungs labouring) and had run into the next room, which the lodgers, pres-
sured by the father, were already approaching more rapidly.
One could observe how under the sister's practiced hands the
sheets and pillows on the beds were thrown on high and arranged. Even before the lodgers had reached the room, she
was finished fixing the beds and was slipping out. The father
seemed so gripped once again with his stubbornness that he
forgot about the respect which he always owed to his renters.
He pressed on and on, until at the door of the room the
middle gentleman stamped loudly with his foot and thus
brought the father to a standstill. "I hereby declare," the
middle lodger said, raising his hand and casting his glance
both on the mother and the sister, "that considering the dis-
graceful conditions prevailing in this apartment and family,"
with this he spat decisively on the floor, "I immediately cancel
my room. I will, of course, pay nothing at all for the days
which I have lived here; on the contrary I shall think about
whether or not I will initiate some sort of action against you,
something which--believe me-- will be very easy to establish."
He fell silent and looked directly in front of him, as if he was
waiting for something. In fact, his two friends immediately
joined in with their opinions, "We also give immediate notice." At that he seized the door handle, banged the door
shut, and locked it.

The father groped his way tottering to his chair and let
himself fall in it. It looked as if he was stretching out for his
usual evening snooze, but the heavy nodding of his head
(which looked as if it was without support) showed that he
was not sleeping at all. Gregor had lain motionless the entire

time in the spot where the lodgers had caught him. Disappointment with the collapse of his plan and perhaps also his weakness brought on his severe hunger made it impossible for him to move. He was certainly afraid that a general disaster would break over him at any moment, and he waited. He was not even startled when the violin fell from the mother's lap, out from under her trembling fingers, and gave off a reverberating tone.

"My dear parents," said the sister banging her hand on the table by way of an introduction, "things cannot go on any longer in this way. Maybe if you don't understand that, well, I do. I will not utter my brother's name in front of this monster, and thus I say only that we must try to get rid of it. We have tried what is humanly possible to take care of it and to be patient. I believe that no one can criticize us in the slightest." "She is right in a thousand ways," said the father to himself. The mother, who was still incapable of breathing properly, began to cough numbly with her hand held up over her mouth and a manic expression in her eyes.

The sister hurried over to her mother and held her forehead. The sister's words seemed to have led the father to certain reflections. He sat upright, played with his uniform hat among the plates, which still lay on the table from the lodgers' evening meal, and looked now and then at the motionless Gregor.

"We must try to get rid of it," the sister now said decisively to the father, for the mother, in her coughing fit, wasn't listening to anything, "it is killing you both. I see it coming. When people have to work as hard as we all do, they cannot also tolerate this endless torment at home. I just can't go on any more." And she broke out into such a crying fit that her tears flowed out down onto her mother's face. She wiped them off her mother with mechanical motions of her hands.

"Child," said the father sympathetically and with obvious appreciation, "then what should we do?"

The sister only shrugged her shoulders as a sign of the perplexity which, in contrast to her previous confidence, had come over her while she was crying.

"If only he understood us," said the father in a semi-questioning tone. The sister, in the midst of her sobbing, shook her hand energetically as a sign that there was no point thinking of that.

"If he only understood us," repeated the father and by shutting his eyes he absorbed the sister's conviction of the impossibility of this point, "then perhaps some compromise would be possible with him. But as it is. . ."

"It must be gotten rid of," cried the sister; "That is the only way, father. You must try to get rid of the idea that this is Gregor. The fact that we have believed for so long, that is truly our real misfortune. But how can it be Gregor? If it were Gregor, he would have long ago realized that a communal life among human beings is not possible with such an animal and would have gone away voluntarily. Then we would not have a brother, but we could go on living and honour his memory. But this animal plagues us. It drives away the lodgers, will obviously take over the entire apartment, and leave us to spend the night in the alley. Just look, father," she suddenly cried out, "he's already starting up again." With a fright which was totally incomprehensible to Gregor, the sister even left the mother, pushed herself away from her chair, as if she would sooner sacrifice her mother than remain in Gregor's vicinity, and rushed behind her father who, excited merely by her behaviour, also stood up and half raised his arms in front of the sister as though to protect her.

But Gregor did not have any notion of wishing to create problems for anyone and certainly not for his sister. He had just started to turn himself around in order to creep back into his room, quite a startling sight, since, as a result of his suffering condition, he had to guide himself through the difficulty of turning around with his head, in this process lifting and banging it against the floor several times. He paused and looked around. His good intentions seem to have been recognized. The fright had only lasted for a moment. Now they looked at him in silence and sorrow. His mother lay in her chair, with her legs stretched out and pressed together; her eyes were almost shut from weariness. The father and sister sat next to one another. The sister had set her hands around the father's neck.

" Now perhaps I can actually turn myself around," thought Gregor and began the task again. He couldn't stop puffing at the effort and had to rest now and then.

Besides no one was urging him on. It was all left to him on his own. When he had completed turning around, he immediately began to wander straight back. He was astonished at the great distance which separated him from his room and did not understand in the least how in his weakness he had covered the same distance a short time before, almost without noticing it. Constantly intent only on creeping along quickly, he hardly paid any attention to the fact that no word or cry from his family interrupted him.

Only when he was already in the door did he turn his head, not completely, because he felt his neck growing stiff. At any rate he still saw that behind him nothing had changed. Only the sister was standing up. His last glimpse brushed over the mother who was now completely asleep. Hardly was he inside his room when the door was pushed shut very quickly, bolted fast, and barred. Gregor was startled by the sudden commotion behind him, so much so that his little limbs bent double under him. It was his sister who had been in such a hurry. She had stood up right away, had waited, and had then sprung forward nimbly. Gregor had not heard anything of her approach. She cried out "Finally!" to her parents, as she turned the key in the lock.

"What now?" Gregor asked himself and looked around him in the darkness. He soon made the discovery that he could no longer move at all. He was not surprised at that. On the contrary, it struck him as unnatural that he had really been able up to this point to move around with these thin little legs. Besides he felt relatively content. True, he had pains throughout his entire body, but it seemed to him that they were gradually becoming weaker and weaker and would finally go away completely. The rotten apple in his back and the inflamed surrounding area, entirely covered with white dust, he hardly noticed. He remembered his family with deep feeling and love. In this business, his own thought that he had to disappear was, if possible, even more decisive than his sister's. He remained in this state of empty and peaceful reflection until the tower clock struck three o'clock in the morning. From the window he witnessed the beginning of the general dawning outside. Then without willing it, his head sank all the way down, and from his nostrils flowed out weakly out his last breath.

Early in the morning the cleaning woman came. In her sheer energy and haste she banged all the doors (in precisely the way people had already asked her to avoid), so much so that once she arrived a quiet sleep was no longer possible anywhere in the entire apartment. In her customarily brief visit to Gregor she at first found nothing special. She thought he lay so immobile there intending to play the offended party. She gave him credit for as complete an understanding as possible. Because she happened to hold the long broom in her hand, she tried to tickle Gregor with it from the door. When that was quite unsuccessful, she became irritated and poked Gregor a little, and only when she had shoved him from his place without any resistance did she become attentive. When she quickly realized the true state of affairs, her eyes grew large, she whistled to herself, but didn't restrain herself for long. She pulled open the door of the bedroom and yelled in a loud voice into the darkness, "Come and look. It's kicked the bucket. It's lying there, totally snuffed!"

The Samsa married couple sat upright in their marriage bed and had to get over their fright at the cleaning woman before they managed to grasp her message. But then Mr. and Mrs. Samsa climbed very quickly out of bed, one on either side. Mr. Samsa threw the bedspread over his shoulders, Mrs. Samsa came out only in her night-shirt, and like this they stepped into Gregor's room. Meanwhile the door of the living room (in which Grete had slept since the lodgers had arrived on the scene) had also opened. She was fully clothed, as if she had not slept at all; her white face also seem to indicate that.

"Dead?" said Mrs. Samsa and looked questioningly at the cleaning woman, although she could check everything on her own and even understand without a check. "I should say so," said the cleaning woman and, by way of proof, poked Gregor's body with the broom a considerable distance more to the side. Mrs. Samsa made a movement as if she wished to restrain the broom, but didn't do it. "Well," said Mr. Samsa, "now we can give thanks to God." He crossed himself, and the three women followed his example.

Grete, who did not take her eyes off the corpse, said, "Look how thin he was. He had eaten nothing for such a long time. The meals which came in here came out again exactly the same." In fact, Gregor's body was completely flat and dry. That was apparent really for the first time, now that he was no longer raised on his small limbs and, moreover, now that nothing else distracted one's gaze.

"Grete, come into us for a moment," said Mrs. Samsa with a melancholy smile, and Grete went, not without looking back at the corpse, behind her parents into the bed room. The cleaning woman shut the door and opened the window wide. In spite of the early morning, the fresh air was partly tinged with warmth. It was already the end of March.

The three lodgers stepped out of their room and looked around for their breakfast, astonished that they had been forgotten. "Where is the breakfast?" asked the middle one of the gentlemen grumpily to the cleaning woman. However, she laid her finger to her lips and then quickly and silently indicated to the lodgers that they could come into Gregor's room. So they came and stood around Gregor's corpse, their hands in the pockets of their somewhat worn jackets, in the room, which was already quite bright.

Then the door of the bed room opened, and Mr. Samsa appeared in his uniform, with his wife on one arm and his daughter on the other. All were a little tear stained. Now and then Grete pressed her face onto her father's arm.

"Get out of my apartment immediately," said Mr. Samsa and pulled open the door, without letting go of the women. "What do you mean?" said the middle lodger, somewhat dismayed and with a sugary smile. The two others kept their hands behind them and constantly rubbed them against each other, as if in joyful anticipation of a great squabble which must end up in their favour. "I mean exactly what I say," replied Mr. Samsa and went directly with his two female companions up to the lodger. The latter at first stood there motionless and looked at the floor, as if matters were arranging themselves in a new way in his head. "All right, then we'll go," he said and looked up at Mr. Samsa as if, suddenly overcome by humility, he was asking fresh permission for this decision. Mr. Samsa merely nodded to him repeatedly with his eyes open wide.

Following that, the lodger actually went immediately with long strides into the hall. His two friends had already been listening for a while with their hands quite still, and now they hopped smartly after him, as if afraid that Mr. Samsa could step into the hall ahead of them and disturb their reunion with their leader. In the hall all three of them took their hats from the coat rack, pulled their canes from the cane holder, bowed silently, and left the apartment. In what turned out to be an entirely groundless mistrust, Mr. Samsa stepped with the two women out onto the landing, leaned against the railing, and looked down as the three lodgers slowly but steadily made their way down the long staircase, disappeared on each floor in a certain turn of the stairwell and in a few seconds came out again. The deeper they proceeded, the more the Samsa family lost interest in them, and when a butcher with a tray on his head come to meet them and then with a proud bearing ascended the stairs high above them, Mr. Samsa., together with the women, left the banister, and they all returned, as if relieved, back into their apartment.

They decided to pass that day resting and going for a stroll. Not only had they earned this break from work, but there was no question that they really needed it. And so they sat down at the table and wrote three letters of apology: Mr. Samsa to his supervisor, Mrs. Samsa to her client, and Grete to her proprietor. During the writing the cleaning woman came in to say that she was going off, for her morning work was finished. The three people writing at first merely nodded, without glancing up. Only when the cleaning woman was still unwilling to depart, did they look up angrily. "Well?" asked Mr. Samsa. The cleaning woman stood smiling in the doorway, as if she had a great stroke of luck to report to the family but would only do it if she was asked directly. The almost upright small ostrich feather in her hat, which had irritated Mr. Samsa during her entire service, swayed lightly in all directions. "All right then, what do you really want?" asked Mrs. Samsa, whom the cleaning lady still usually respected. "Well," answered the cleaning woman (smiling so happily she couldn't go on speaking right away), "about how that rubbish from the next room should be thrown out, you mustn't worry about it. It's all taken care of." Mrs. Samsa and Grete bent down to their letters, as though they wanted to go on writing; Mr. Samsa, who noticed that the cleaning woman wanted to start describing everything in detail, decisively prevented her with an outstretched hand. But since she was not allowed to explain, she remembered the great hurry she was in, and called out, clearly insulted, "Ta ta, everyone," turned around furiously and left the apartment with a fearful slamming of the door.

"This evening she'll be let go," said Mr. Samsa, but he got no answer from either his wife or from his daughter, because the cleaning woman seemed to have upset once again the tranquility they had just attained. They got up, went to the window and remained there, with their arms about each other. Mr. Samsa turned around in his chair in their direction and observed them quietly for a while. Then he called out, "All right, come here then. Let's finally get rid of old things. And have a little consideration for me." The women attended to him at once. They rushed to him, caressed him, and quickly ended their letters.

Then all three left the apartment together, something they had not done for months now, and took the electric tram into the open air outside the city. The car in which they were sitting by themselves was totally engulfed by the warm sun. They talked to each other, leaning back comfortably in their seats, about future prospects, and they discovered that on closer observation these were not at all bad, for all three had employment, about which they had not really questioned each other at all, which was extremely favorable and with especially promising prospects. The greatest improvement in their situation at this moment, of course, had to come from a change of dwelling. Now they wanted to rent an apartment smaller and cheaper but better situated and generally more practical than the present one, which Gregor had found. While they amused themselves in this way, it struck Mr. and Mrs. Samsa almost at the same moment how their daughter, who was getting more animated all the time, had blossomed recently, in spite of all the troubles which had made her cheeks pale, into a beautiful and voluptuous young woman. Growing more silent and almost unconsciously understanding each other in their glances, they thought that the time was now at hand to seek out a good honest man for her. And it was something of a confirmation of their new dreams and good intentions when at the end of their journey the daughter first lifted herself up and stretched her young body.

CPSIA information can be obtained
at www.ICGtesting.com
Printed in the USA
LVHW100829120123
736944LV00004B/779